Opening se[...]
of famous m[...]

fitway

Selected by Léon Mazzella

© Fitway Publishing, 2004.
Original editions in French, English, Spanish, Italian.

English language translation by Translate-A-Book, Oxford.

All rights reserved, including partial or complete translation, adaptation and reproduction rights, in any form and for any purpose.

DESIGN AND CREATION: GRAPH'M

ISBN: 2-7528-0112-2
Publisher code: T00112

Copyright registration: 2004 September
Printed in Singapore by Tien Wah Press

www.fitwaypublishing.com
Fitway Publishing – 12, avenue d'Italie – 75627 Paris cedex 13

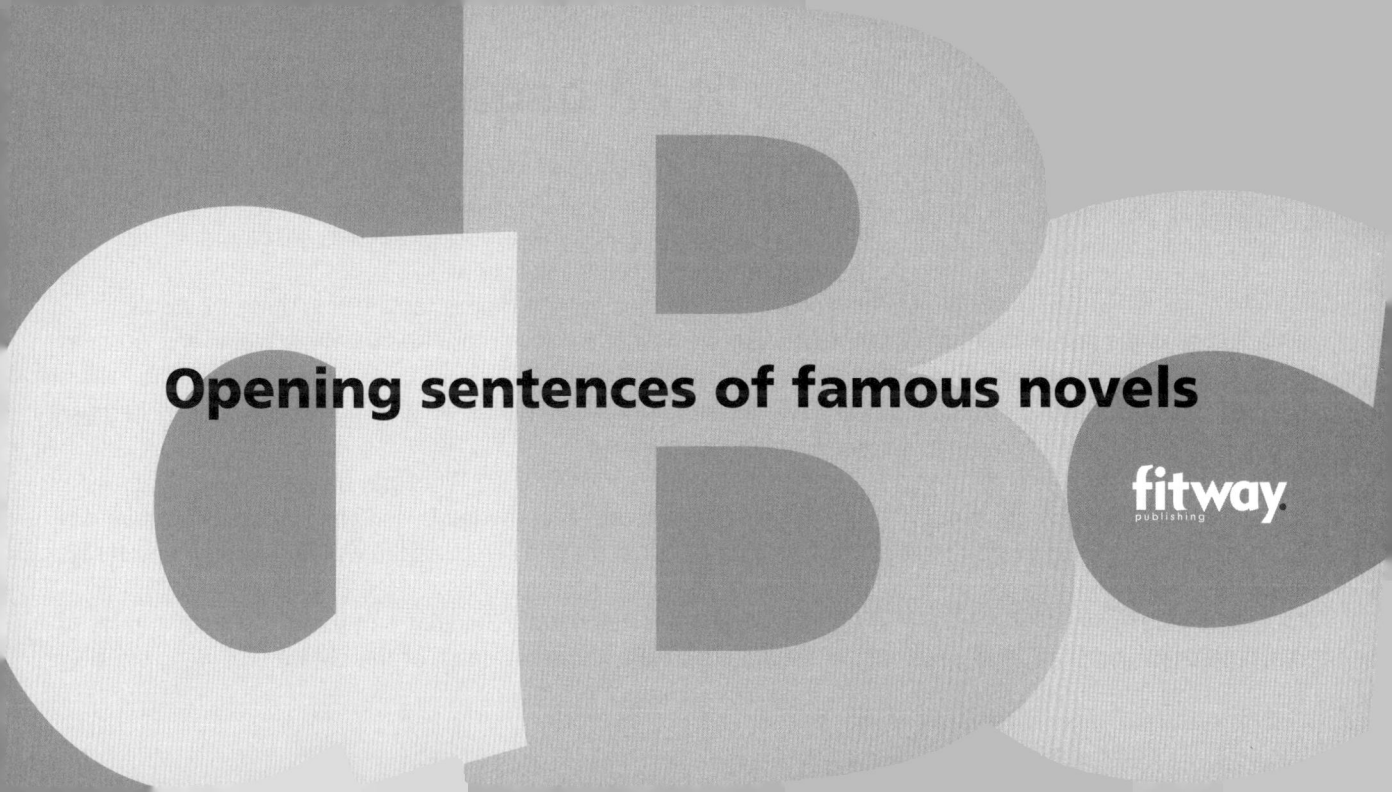

Opening sentences of famous novels

fitway
publishing

'It all began just like that'

It's because the first sentence of a novel is short that it is so meaningful. There are plenty of long sentences too, but they do not figure in this collection, which favours opening lines that are succinct, terse, dazzling.
The short sentence should be the norm.
Take *Journey to the End of the Night*: 'It all began just like that.' All of Céline is contained in those six words.
With Radiguet, the first sentence of *Possessed by the Devil* wonderfully encapsulates what is to come and works as a disturbing aside; a perverse trifle.
The first sentences of novels appearing here were chosen for the international fame of the work they open, because of the author's fame and because they convey something essential.
There is pure literature (Tolstoy, Conrad and Stendhal in appropriate measures). What may be the essence of literature: 'I often look at myself in the mirror' (L-R des Forêts). It is a shame that the fourth sentence of Gide's *Marshlands* (strictly, a 'sotie', a short satirical piece rather than a novel) is not the first: 'I replied: I'm writing *Marshlands*.' It says absolutely everything.
The 'something essential' is a trace of wit (de Luca), humour (Henri Roth, Blondin), surprise mixed with a touch of coarseness (Vargas Llosa), the power of the message (Camus), the shrewdness of the phrase (Fuentes), the silky

aphorism disguised as something more substantial in novel form (Mishima),
the sonorous beauty and the assertion – though lightly done – of a hallmark,
an individual style (Gracq, García Marquez).
There is also the standard sentence, the one you whisper to yourself and
amongst members of the tribe (Maclean! O'Brien to a lesser degree).
The announcement of an ambitious novel (carnal, voluble, romantic, ardent, generous, pompous in places) is contained
in the space of an opening sentence and, by some miracle, it succeeds without going over the top (Cohen).
A well-known piece which it is so pleasant to return to is represented by Proust ('For a long time ...') and Hemingway,
and also by Kafka, Nizan, Cervantes, Flaubert, Nabokov and Eco.
Those sentences go round the world eighty times a day. They are familiar to every *aficionado* in every language. The
magic of the literary journey!
The first sentence of a novel has a strange fugitive power. It sketches, provokes, captures, binds or dives into a muffled
fade. It is never disinterested: it intends to *say* something.
From Zweig to Grass or Aragon, we sail on from the narrative beauty to the hard idea embedded in the style. Two
worlds. Three sentences, three authors out of thousands, three novels, three major works.

This little book can serve as a kaleidoscope, a protean anthology, a fount of dreams or a firework display: literature is one of the most colourful things in the world.

The immediacy of a novel's first sentence can be astounding. It's the one we expect most from.

It is the face, the first look at the first meeting. It is easy to fall in love with it.

It can be determining, showing the way in. The ones you are going to read are all, to a greater or lesser extent, invitations to a journey, either real or metaphorical (Delibes, Gary). They are the admission tickets for the works. The opener has no quotation marks; access is free.

You may like to guess which books these sentences are from: the titles of the books can be found at the back of the book! To start with, we give you the sentence and its author.

Read, savour and enjoy yourself. That is partly what literature is for. You want to start now? OK: 'In the beginning was the Word and the Word was with God, and the Word was God.'

For a literary 'chat', you can find us on fitwaypublishing.com ...

L. M.

OPENING SENTENCES OF FAMOUS NOVELS **7**

He was an old man who fished alone in a skiff in the Gulf Stream and he had gone eighty-four days now without taking a fish.

Ernest Hemingway

8 OPENING SENTENCES OF FAMOUS NOVELS

As Gregor Samsa awoke one morning from uneasy dreams he found himself transformed in his bed into a gigantic insect.

Franz Kafka

OPENING SENTENCES OF FAMOUS NOVELS **9**

My first act on entering this world was to kill my mother.

William Boyd

10 OPENING SENTENCES OF FAMOUS NOVELS

In the beginning was the Word and the Word was with God, and the Word was God.

Umberto Eco

OPENING SENTENCES OF FAMOUS NOVELS **11**

Mother died today.

Albert Camus

12 OPENING SENTENCES OF FAMOUS NOVELS

Once his train had passed the suburbs and smoke of Charleville, it seemed to Officer Cadet Grange that the ugliness of the world was melting away: he became aware that not a single house was to be seen.

Julien Gracq

OPENING SENTENCES OF FAMOUS NOVELS **13**

One September morning, Giovanni Drogo, being newly commissioned, set out from the city for Fort Bastiani; it was his first posting.

Dino Buzzati

14 OPENING SENTENCES OF FAMOUS NOVELS

Behind the screen of bushes which surrounded the spring, Popeye watched the man drinking.

William Faulkner

OPENING SENTENCES OF FAMOUS NOVELS 15

On an exceptionally hot evening early in July a young man came slowly out of the garret in which he lodged in S. Place and walked slowly, as though in hesitation, towards K. Bridge.

Fyodor Dostoevsky

In a village of La Mancha, the name of which I purposely omit, there lived, not long ago, one of those gentlemen who usually keep a lance on a rack, an old target, a lean horse, and a greyhound for coursing.

Miguel de Cervantes

OPENING SENTENCES OF FAMOUS NOVELS 17

In the corner of a first-class smoking carriage, Mr Justice Wargrave, lately retired from the bench, puffed at a cigar and ran an interested eye through the political news in The Times.

Agatha Christie

18 OPENING SENTENCES OF FAMOUS NOVELS

In eighteenth-century France there lived a man who was one of the most gifted and abominable personages in an era that knew no lack of gifted and abominable personages.

Patrick Süskind

At an age when most young Scotsmen were lifting skirts, plowing furrows and spreading seed, Mungo Park was displaying his bare buttocks to al-haj' Ali Ibn Fatoudi, Emir of Ludamar.

T C Boyle

20 OPENING SENTENCES OF FAMOUS NOVELS

You all know the wild grief that besets us when we remember times of happiness.

Ernst Jünger

One day, I was already old, in the entrance of a public place a man came up to me.

Marguerite Duras

22 OPENING SENTENCES OF FAMOUS NOVELS

A wave curled and running up the wet foreshore licked Robinson's toes as he lay face down on the sand.

Michel Tournier

That night – like so many other nights that you couldn't think straight about them – Térii the Narrator walked with measured steps along the sacred square.

Victor Segalen

24 OPENING SENTENCES OF FAMOUS NOVELS

I am going to get into a lot of trouble.

Raymond Radiguet

OPENING SENTENCES OF FAMOUS NOVELS

Many years later, as he faced the firing squad, Colonel Aureliano Buendia was to remember that distant afternoon when his father took him to discover ice.

Gabriel Garcia Marquez

26 OPENING SENTENCES OF FAMOUS NOVELS

When Esther, Pelé's wife, went to fetch a few armfuls of hay for the clients' horses, she stumbled over the body of a young Indian woman by the millstone.

Francisco Coloane

OPENING SENTENCES OF FAMOUS NOVELS **27**

The crowd stood up as if it were all one person.

Jorge Amado

28 OPENING SENTENCES OF FAMOUS NOVELS

All has become quiet in Moscow.

Count L N Tolstoy

When I was young, I sometimes stared suddenly at the face of an unknown man and asked myself: what if this gentleman was *my father*?

Mircea Eliade

30 OPENING SENTENCES OF FAMOUS NOVELS

On the 15th of May 1796, General Bonaparte made his entry into Milan at the head of that young army which shortly before had crossed the Bridge of Lodi and taught the world that after all these centuries Caesar and Alexander had a successor.

Marie Henri Beyle (Stendhal)

OPENING SENTENCES OF FAMOUS NOVELS **31**

For a long time I used to go to bed early.

Marcel Proust

32 OPENING SENTENCES OF FAMOUS NOVELS

Stately, plump Buck Milligan came from the stairhead, bearing a bowl of lather on which a mirror and a razor lay crossed.

James Joyce

He was an inch, perhaps two, under six feet, powerfully built, and he advanced straight at you with a slight stoop of the shoulders, head forward, and a fixed from-under stare which made you think of a charging bull.

Joseph Conrad

When Tommy Salter, Lester Hoenig, and the Hayden brothers left Bentrock, Montana, at dawn, only a gentle snow — flakes fat as bits of white cloth — fell from the November sky.

Larry Watson

OPENING SENTENCES OF FAMOUS NOVELS **35**

No bondage is worse than the hope of happiness.

Carlos Fuentes

36 OPENING SENTENCES OF FAMOUS NOVELS

Shaw used to be a model, but she is still beautiful, both wild and shy, like a coyote or wild dog – more beautiful in fact than when she was a model.

Rick Bass

OPENING SENTENCES OF FAMOUS NOVELS **37**

It was the summer that men first walked on the moon.

Paul Auster

38 OPENING SENTENCES OF FAMOUS NOVELS

The sea is high again today, with a thrilling flush of wind.

Lawrence Durrell

OPENING SENTENCES OF FAMOUS NOVELS **39**

He came into my life in February 1932 and never left it again.

Fred Uhlman

40 OPENING SENTENCES OF FAMOUS NOVELS

> Over two months elapsed before Des Esseintes could immerse himself in the peaceful silence of his house at Fontenay, for purchases of all sorts still kept him perambulating the streets and ransacking the shops from one end of Paris to the other.

Joris-Karl Huysmans

The studio was filled with the rich odour of roses, and when the light summer wind stirred amidst the trees of the garden, there came through the open door the heavy scent of the lilac, or the more delicate perfume of the pink-flowering thorn.

Oscar Wilde

42 OPENING SENTENCES OF FAMOUS NOVELS

I was twenty years old. I defy anyone to say that this is the best time of your life.

Paul Nizan

Candles burning in silver candelabra were reflected in the bowls of crystal cognac glasses.

Arturo Perez-Reverte

It was five o'clock in the morning, it was raining, and Eric von Lhomond, who had been wounded at Saragossa and treated on board the Italian hospital ship, was waiting in the buffet of Pisa station for the train which would take him back to Germany.

Marguerite Yourcenar

OPENING SENTENCES OF FAMOUS NOVELS 45

Two mountain chains traverse the republic roughly from north to south, forming between them a number of valleys and plateaux.

Malcolm Lowry

46 OPENING SENTENCES OF FAMOUS NOVELS

The first time that Aurélien saw Bérénice, she struck him as decidedly plain.

Louis Aragon

OPENING SENTENCES OF FAMOUS NOVELS 47

Since I was very young, I have been fascinated by the migrations of wild animals.

Dan O'Brien

48 OPENING SENTENCES OF FAMOUS NOVELS

Fish is only fish once it's in the boat.

Erri De Luca

OPENING SENTENCES OF FAMOUS NOVELS **49**

*'Sons of bitches,'
Lituma felt the vomit rising in his throat.*

Mario Vargas Llosa

50 OPENING SENTENCES OF FAMOUS NOVELS

Mrs Dalloway said she would buy the flowers herself.

Virginia Woolf

OPENING SENTENCES OF FAMOUS NOVELS 51

There were five of them, mighty-shouldered fellows, round a table drinking, in a gloomy sort of room which smelt of brine and the sea.

Pierre Loti

52 OPENING SENTENCES OF FAMOUS NOVELS

For Christmas I wanted a rat, as I was looking for the key words for a poem about the education of the human race.

Günter Grass

In the spring of 1917, when Doctor Richard Diver first arrived in Zurich, he was twenty-six years old, a fine age for a man, indeed the very acme of bachelorhood.

F Scott Fitzgerald

54 OPENING SENTENCES OF FAMOUS NOVELS

For many years I claimed I could remember things seen at the time of my own birth.

Yukio Mishima

All of this happened while I was walking around starving in Christiana – that strange city no one escapes from until it has left its mark on him...

Knut Hamsun

56 OPENING SENTENCES OF FAMOUS NOVELS

I had a farm in Africa beneath the Ngong.

Karen Blixen

Wonderful or supernatural events are not so uncommon, rather they are irregular in their incidence.

David Garnett

58 OPENING SENTENCES OF FAMOUS NOVELS

I often look at myself in the mirror.

Louis-René des Forêts

Count d'Olavidez had not yet established foreign settlements in the Sierra Morena – that lofty chain of mountains that separates Andalusia from La Mancha – which at that time was inhabited solely by smugglers, bandits and a few gypsies who had the reputation of eating the travellers they murdered, whence the source of the Spanish proverb: *'Las gitanas de Sierra Morena quieren carne de hombres.'*

Jean Potocki

60 OPENING SENTENCES OF FAMOUS NOVELS

I am in my mother's room.

Samuel Beckett

It is hard, despicable even, to avert your eyes from those of a man who is bleeding to death; but it is even harder to hold his gaze while trying to delve into the maelstrom of confused passions and deathbed secrets racing across his retinas.

Juan Manuel de Prada

62 OPENING SENTENCES OF FAMOUS NOVELS

It is easy to forget that in the main we die only seven times more slowly than our dogs.

Jim Harrison

In our family, there was no clear line between religion and fly fishing.

Norman Maclean

64 OPENING SENTENCES OF FAMOUS NOVELS

In Alsace, around 1850, a teacher overburdened with children agreed to become a grocer.

Jean-Paul Sartre

OPENING SENTENCES OF FAMOUS NOVELS **65**

Long after their usual time, the wild boar were still coming to drink at the deserted pool.

Roger Nimier

66 OPENING SENTENCES OF FAMOUS NOVELS

I am young, rich and cultured; and I am unhappy.

Fritz Zorn

There were the usual last-minute comings and goings on the big steamship which was due to leave New York at midnight for Buenos Aires.

Stefan Zweig

68 OPENING SENTENCES OF FAMOUS NOVELS

I yield to your desire.

Honoré de Balzac

OPENING SENTENCES OF FAMOUS NOVELS **69**

He dismounted and strode past hazel and briar, followed by the two horses which the valet led by the reins, through the crackling silence, stripped to the waist under the noonday sun, smiling as he went, a strange, princely figure, confident of coming victory.

Albert Cohen

70 OPENING SENTENCES OF FAMOUS NOVELS

Barcelona is a city of six hundred thousand two hundred souls, and it only has one public urinal.

Henry de Montherlant

OPENING SENTENCES OF FAMOUS NOVELS 71

The appeared, as in a dream, on top of the dune, half hidden by the cloud of sand kicked up by their feet.

Jean-Marie Gustave Le Clézio

72 OPENING SENTENCES OF FAMOUS NOVELS

It all began just like that.

Louis-Ferdinand Céline

OPENING SENTENCES OF FAMOUS NOVELS **73**

Had he pulled at my eyelids to find out what they concealed?

Joseph Kessel

Every evening, Lorenzo found himself back in front of the eight male nude statues decorating the entrance to the park.

Ramon Gomez de la Serna

OPENING SENTENCES OF FAMOUS NOVELS 75

The winter sun, poor ghost of itself, hung milky and wan behind layers of cloud above the huddled roofs of the town.

Thomas Mann

76 OPENING SENTENCES OF FAMOUS NOVELS

It was at Megara, a suburb of Carthage, in the gardens of Hamilcar.

Gustave Flaubert

Do not try, Nathaniel, to find God *here* or *there* – but everywhere.

André Gide

78 OPENING SENTENCES OF FAMOUS NOVELS

At that time I was squandering my Venezuelan legacy.

Patrick Modiano

The story had held us, round the fire, sufficiently breathless, but except the obvious remark that it was gruesome, as on Christmas Eve in an old house a strange tale should essentially be, I remember no comment uttered till someone happened to note it as the only case he had met in which such a visitation had fallen on a child.

Henry James

80 OPENING SENTENCES OF FAMOUS NOVELS

Mr Jones, of the Manor Farm, had locked the hen-houses for the night, but was too drunk to remember to shut the pop-holes.

George Orwell

On a green hillside, a beautiful tree-covered slope where nightingales sang, a group of young men were out walking; they were scarcely more than boys, full of the energy and vitality of a life only just begun.

Adalbert Stifter

82 OPENING SENTENCES OF FAMOUS NOVELS

The sky, a swollen ass's belly, hung very low and threatening over people's heads.

Luis Sepulveda

The *Hamburg*, a three-master,
a rowing and sailing galleass designed
for coastal navigation, with its fine lines and an
overall length of five ells, slipped slowly from the
mouth of the river and headed for the high seas.

Miguel Delibes

84 OPENING SENTENCES OF FAMOUS NOVELS

In my nostrils I can still smell the smoking grease on the burning machine gun.

Mario Rigoni Stern

She was so deeply embedded in my consciousness that for the first year of school I seem to have believed that each of my teachers was my mother in disguise.

Philip Roth

86 OPENING SENTENCES OF FAMOUS NOVELS

The one opened the door with a latch-key and went in, followed by a young fellow who awkwardly removed his cap.

Jack London

OPENING SENTENCES OF FAMOUS NOVELS **87**

Dawn caught Angelo dumb and blissful but awake.

Jean Giono

88 OPENING SENTENCES OF FAMOUS NOVELS

Standing before the kitchen sink and regarding the bright faucets that gleamed so far away, each with a bead of water at its nose, slowly swelling, falling, David again became aware that this world had been created without thought of him.

Henry Roth

Ever since dawn the track had followed the hillside through a tangle of bamboos and elephant grass, in which horse and rider disappeared completely; then the Jesuit's head would reappear above the yellow sea, with his big bony nose jutting out above manly, smiling lips, and with those piercing eyes whose expression suggested wide horizons rather than the pages of a breviary.

Romain Gary

It was five o'clock in the afternoon, or just a little later – the big hand having shifted slightly to the right – when, on the 16th January, Madame Monde, accompanied by an icy draught, burst into the common room of the police commissariat.

Georges Simenon

OPENING SENTENCES OF FAMOUS NOVELS 91

When you said to Doctor Peyrolles that you really did need a belt to keep up your trousers, he replied that savages didn't wear them and they never suffered from varicose veins.

Alexandre Vialatte

It should be sufficient to say that I am Juan Pablo Castel, the painter who killed María Iribarne; I imagine that the trial is still in everyone's mind and that no further information about myself is necessary.

Ernesto Sábato

OPENING SENTENCES OF FAMOUS NOVELS 93

Every other night, Albert Quentin sailed down the Yangtse Kiang in his bed-boat: nearly two thousand miles to the estuary, twenty-six days on the river unless you ran into pirates, a double ration of rice alcohol if the Chinese crew didn't mutiny.

Antoine Blondin

94 OPENING SENTENCES OF FAMOUS NOVELS

Lolita, light of my life, fire of my loins.

Vladimir Nabokov

List of books quoted

- p. 7 Ernest Hemingway, *The Old Man and the Sea*, Jonathan Cape, 1952.
- p. 8 Franz Kafka, *Metamorphosis*, Penguin, 1961.
- p. 9 William Boyd, *The New Confessions*, Penguin, 1988.
- p. 10 Umberto Eco, *In the Name of the Rose*, Vintage, 1998.
- p. 11 Albert Camus, *The Outsider*, Hamish Hamilton, 1960.
- p. 12 Julien Gracq, *A Balcony in the Forest*, Corti, 1958.
- p. 13 Dino Buzzati, *The Tartar Steppe*, Carcanet, 1985.
- p. 14 William Faulkner, *Sanctuary*, The Library of America, 1985.
- p. 15 Fyodor Dostoevsky, *Crime and Punishment*, Dent Dutton, 1958.
- p. 16 Miguel de Cervantes, *The Life and Exploits of the Ingenious Gentleman Don Quixote de la Mancha*, S A and H Oddy, 1809.
- p. 17 Agatha Christie, *And Then There Were None* (formerly *Ten Little Niggers*), HarperCollins, 2001.
- p. 18 Patrick Süskind, *Perfume*, Hamish Hamilton, 1986.
- p. 19 T Coraghessan Boyle, *Water Music*, Victor Gollancz, 1982.
- p. 20 Ernst Jünger, *On the Marble Cliffs*, John Lehmann, 1947.
- p. 21 Marguerite Duras, *The Lover*, Collins, 1985.
- p. 22 Michel Tournier, *Friday or The Other Island*, Collins, 1969.
- p. 23 Victor Segalen (Max Anély), *The Immemorial Ones*, Le Mercure de France, 1907.
- p. 24 Raymond Radiguet, *Possessed by the Devil*, Grasset, 1923.
- p. 25 Gabriel Garcia Marquez, *One Hundred Years of Solitude*, Jonathan Cape, 1970.
- p. 26 Francisco Coloane, *The Simpleton*, Zigzag, 1981.
- p. 27 Jorge Amado, *Jubiabá*, Avon Books, 1984.
- p. 28 Count L N Tolstoy, *The Cossacks*, Sampson Low, Morton, Searle & Rivington, 1878.
- p. 29 Mircea Eliade, *Wedding in Paradise*, 1938.
- p. 30 Marie Henri Beyle (Stendhal), *The Charterhouse of Parma*, Chatto & Windus, 1926.
- p. 31 Marcel Proust, *Swann's Way (Remembrance of Things Past)*, Penguin, 1957.
- p. 32 James Joyce, *Ulysses*, The Odyssey Press, 1932.
- p. 33 Joseph Conrad, *Lord Jim*, J M Dent & Sons Ltd, 1917.
- p. 34 Larry Watson, 'Outside the Jurisdiction (1924)' from *Justice*, Washington Square Press, 1995.
- p. 35 Carlos Fuentes, *Diana: the Goddess Who Hunts Alone*, Bloomsbury, 1995.
- p. 36 Rick Bass, *Platte River*, Houghton Miflin Co / Seymour Lawrence Inc, 1993.
- p. 37 Paul Auster, *Moon Palace*, Faber and Faber, 1989.
- p. 38 Lawrence Durrell, *Justine* (Alexandria Quartet), Faber, 1961.
- p. 39 Fred Uhlman, *Reunion*, Adam Books, 1971.
- p. 40 Joris-Karl Huysmans, *Against Nature*, Penguin, 1966.
- p. 41 Oscar Wilde, *The Picture of Dorian Gray*, Dent Dutton 1955.
- p. 42 Paul Nizan, *Aden Arabia*, Rieder, 1931.
- p. 43 Arturo Perez-Reverte, *The Fencing Master*, Mondadori, 1988.
- p. 44 Marguerite Yourcenar, *The Coup de Grâce*, Gallimard, 1939.
- p. 45 Malcolm Lowry, *Under the Volcano*, Penguin, 1962.
- p. 46 Louis Aragon, *Aurélien*, Pilot Press Ltd, 1946.
- p. 47 Dan O'Brien, *The Rites of Autumn: A Falconer's Journey Across The American West*, Grove Press / Atlantic Monthly Press, 1988.

p. 48 Erri De Luca, *You, Me,* Giangiacomo Feltrinelli Editore, 1988.
p. 49 Maria Vargas Llosa, *Who Killed Palomino Molero,* Faber and Faber, 1988.
p. 50 Virginia Woolf, *Mrs Dalloway,* The Zodiac Press, 1947.
p. 51 Pierre Loti, *Iceland Fisherman,* J M Dent & Sons Ltd, 1935.
p. 52 Günter Grass, *The Rat,* Hermann Luchterhand Verlag, 1986.
p. 53 F Scott Fitzgerald, *Tender Is The Night,* Penguin, 1955.
p. 54 Yukio Mishima, *Confessions of a Mask,* Peter Owen, 1960.
p. 55 Knut Hamsun, *Hunger,* Picador, 1976.
p. 56 Karen Blixen, *Out of Africa,* 1937.
p. 57 David Garnett, *Lady into Fox,* Chatto & Windus, 1922.
p. 58 Louis-René des Forêts, *The Chatterbox,* Gallimard, 1946.
p. 59 Jean Potocki, *The Saragossa Manuscript,* Cassell, 1962.
p. 60 Samuel Beckett, *Molloy,* Grove Press Inc, 1976.
p. 61 Juan Manuel de Prada, *The Tempest,* Sceptre, 2000.
p. 62 Jim Harrison, *The Road Home,* Picador, 1999.
p. 63 Norman Maclean, *A River Runs Through It,* University of Chicago Press, 1976.
p. 64 Jean-Paul Sartre, *Words,* Gallimard, 1964.
p. 65 Roger Nimier, *The Sad Children,* Gallimard, 1951.
p. 66 Fritz Zorn, *Mars,* Kindler Verlag GmbH, 1977.
p. 67 Stefan Zweig, *The Chess Player,* Bermann-Fischer Verlag AB, Stockholm, 1944.
p. 68 Honoré de Balzac, *The Lily in the Valley,* Werdet, 1836.
p. 69 Albert Cohen, *Belle du Seigneur,* Penguin Books, 1995.
p. 70 Henry de Montherlant, *The Little Infanta of Castile,* Gallimard, 1929.
p. 71 Jean-Marie Gustave Le Clézio, *Desert,* Gallimard, 1980.
p. 72 Louis-Ferdinand Céline, *Journey to the End of the Night,* Chatto & Windus, 1934.
p. 73 Joseph Kessel, *The Lion,* Rupert Hart-Davis, 1959.
p. 74 Ramon Gomez de la Serna, *The Amber Woman,* 1927.
p. 75 Thomas Mann, *Tonio Kröger,* Penguin, 1955.
p. 76 Gustave Flaubert, *Salammbô,* Dent Dutton, 1969.
p. 77 André Gide, *Fruits of the Earth,* Vintage, 2002.
p. 78 Patrick Modiano, *The Place de l'Etoile,* Gallimard, 1968.
p. 79 Henry James, *The Turn of the Screw,* 1898.
p. 80 George Orwell, *Animal Farm,* Martin Secker & Warburg, 1945.
p. 81 Adalbert Stifter, *The Recluse,* Jonathan Cape, 1973.
p. 82 Luis Sepulveda, *The Old Man Who Read Love Stories,* Docteur Ray-Güd-Mertin Literarische Agentur, 1991.
p. 83 Miguel Delibes, *The Heretic,* Destino, 1998.
p. 84 Mario Rigoni Stern, *The Sergeant in the Snow,* Giulio Einaudi, 1953.
p. 85 Philip Roth, *Portnoy's Complaint,* Corgi Books, 1971.
p. 86 Jack London, *Martin Eden,* William Heinemann, 1910.
p. 87 Jean Giono, *The Hussar on the Roof,* Gallimard, 1951.
p. 88 Henry Roth, *Call It Sleep,* Michael Joseph, 1963.
p. 89 Romain Gary, *The Roots of Heaven,* Michael Joseph, 1958.
p. 90 Georges Simenon, *The Flight of Monsieur Monde,* Omnibus, 2002.
p. 91 Alexandre Vialatte, *Fruits of the Congo,* Gallimard, 1951.
p. 92 Ernesto Sabato, *The Tunnel,* Jonathan Cape, 1968.
p. 93 Antoine Blondin, *A Monkey in Winter,* W H Allen, 1960.
p. 94 Vladimir Nabokov, *Lolita,* Weidenfeld & Nicolson, 1959.